Echoes of Grace

A Collection of Poetry, Art, and Faith by Melissa "Missy" Bishop

"But grow in Grace and in the knowledge of our Lord and Savior, Jesus Christ." 2 Peter 3:18

Melissa "Missy" Bishop

Echoes of Grace

By Melissa "Missy" Bishop

Copyright © 2016

All rights reserved.

Printed in the United States of America. No part of this book may be used or reproduced in any manner whatsoever without written permission except in the case of brief quotations embodied in critical articles and reviews. All people and facts in this book are fictions. Any resemblance to real people or facts is coincidental. Scripture quotations are taken from the Holy Bible, New Living Translation, copyright ©1996, 2004, 2007, 2013, 2015 by Tyndale House Foundation. Used by permission of Tyndale House Publishers, Inc., Carol Stream, Illinois 60188. All rights reserved.

Snow Dragon Publishing

Ashland, OH. 44803

First Printing 2016

Cover design by Abigail Mendell

Printed on acid-free paper

Library of Congress Control No: 2016944268
ISBN: 978-0-9971429-2-1

Snow Dragon 2016

Melissa "Missy" Bishop

Acknowledgements

So many people helped me throughout the process of getting this book ready for publication. From the first time I sat down with a blank page in front of me to the completion of each poem and sketch in between, this labor of love would not have happened without each of you! I am truly humbled at the outpouring of love and support I received when the Lord laid this project on my heart.

I want to thank my husband, Gary, for your encouraging words and support throughout the process. All the times I felt like giving up, you offered those words of encouragement that helped get me on the right track again. I want to thank my siblings for reading much of the poems and offering pointers with grammar, wording, etc., as well as offering ideas for the sketches some of the poems needed. Many thanks to both my mom and my friend, Lisa Robertson, for the time you both spent in helping with the editing process and getting it looking great!

Thank you to Pastor Ray Hurt for taking time out of your busy schedule to write such an amazing forward for my book! I am overwhelmed and truly humbled by the words you penned. Many thanks to my mentor, Joseph Lumpkin, for the advice and guidance you provided in getting this book ready for publication.

And, last but not least, to the rest of my family, my friends, my church family and my Shinsei Hapkido family for the advice and support each of you offered. May God bless each and every one of you!

I also want to credit a few different contributors from whose photographs or art inspired a number of the sketches completed for this work, including Bigstockphoto.com contributors Clearviewstock, Chaoss, Yastremska, Imarin, Photoeuphoria, Balaikin2009, Subbotina Anna, Anpet2000, Ivnel, Conrado, Brickrena, Mikdam and Melpomene. Also, I'd like to recognize "Crystal Evening" by Kagaya for the inspiration for "Divine", and "Valley of the Shadow of Death" by Robson Batista at deviantart.com for the inspiration for "Valley." And last but not least, I want to thank Jenna Miller for being my live model inspiration for "Undone".

Melissa "Missy" Bishop

Table of Contents

Dedication	9	21. Almost	79
Forward	11	22. It is Finished	83
1. Echoes of Grace	13	23. Valley	87
2. Divine	16	24. Healing	90
3. Gaze	19	25. Scars	93
4. Heartbeats	22	26. Hope	96
5. Selah	25	27. Undone	99
6. My Father's Eyes	29	28. All Things New	103
7. Dawn of Grace	33	29. Above the Waves	106
8. Lifeline	36	30. My Prayer	110
9. Wanderer	39	31. Embrace	114
10. Rescue	43	32. Peace	117
11. Shinsei	46	33. Tapestry	120
12. Warrior	49	34. Dancing in the Light	123
13. Treasure	52	35. Saturated with Grace	126
14. A Mother's Prayers	55	36. Two Hearts	129
15. For the Love of a Child	59	37. I Love You More	132
16. The Sweet Sound of Silence	62	38. A Place that I Envision	135
17. He Came	65	39. Come Away	138
18. Hero	68	40. Reminders	142
19. Grace and Truth	72	41. Realm of No Shadows	145
20. Glimpses of Glory	76		

Melissa "Missy" Bishop

Dedication

This book is lovingly and humbly dedicated to every wounded soul who deigns to read it. May the scriptures, prose and art contained herein bless you and encourage you in this walk of faith. I want you to know that you are not alone. Whatever struggle, whatever trial, whatever the enemy has brought against you, there is someone else who has been through the same thing and has come through the fire. Keep your eyes on Jesus, dear ones. Keep hold of His hand. He will never leave you. He will never forsake you.

And as always, I pray that through this work that the Lord's name is glorified and lifted up. To Him alone be the glory forever and ever!

Melissa "Missy" Bishop

Forward

Through the years I have met many people who claimed an intimate relationship with God, but quite often the evidence of such a relationship failed to be evident. Missy Bishop is one of the people who demonstrate in their everyday lives that their spirit has made contact with Divine inspiration. Her poetry reveals a heart for the person and presence of someone higher and holier than normal humanity.

I am honored to recommend her inspired writings. Her poetry will reveal the essence of the Divine and bring the reader closer to an understanding of who God really is to them.

Read her inspired poetry in a quiet safe place and listen for the voice of God!

Dr. Ray E. Hurt
Senior Pastor
Princeton Church of God and Lifeline Church

Melissa "Missy" Bishop

Echoes of Grace

"I will bring that group through the fire and make them pure.

I will refine them like silver and purify them like gold.

They will call on my name, and I will answer them.

I will say, 'These are my people, and they will say, 'The LORD is our God.'"

Zechariah 13:9

"Rather, you must grow in the grace and knowledge of our Lord and Savior Jesus Christ.

All glory to him, both now and forever! Amen."

2 Peter 3:18

"He must become greater and greater, and I must become less and less."

John 3:30

"…be strong through the grace that God gives you in Christ Jesus."

2 Timothy 2:1

Melissa "Missy" Bishop

Through the steely façade held firmly in place,

The child within You see.

Though others be fooled by the mask I adorn—

You see to the heart of me.

It is said the trials that deal us wounds

Make stronger those who persist.

And as fire purifies gold that's tried--

So too, struggles refine the earnest.

For Your desire is that I continue to grow—

Both in the Grace and knowledge of You.

And tho' this refiner's fire intolerable seems,

Your strength is what pulls me through.

For through these trials, relentless

The undesired dross burns free.

And the more You form me to Yourself

The more glory can shine through me.

For I must decrease, my strength made weak

In order that others may see--

Echoes of Grace come pouring down,

The heart of the Father perceived.

Divine

"The heavens proclaim the glory of God.

The skies display his craftsmanship."

Psalm 19:1

"When I look at the night sky and see the work of your fingers—

The moon and the stars you set in place—

what are mere mortals that you should think about them,

Human beings that you should care for them?"

Psalm 8:3-4

Gazing skyward at the vast display of splendor,

Spreading across the majestic, celestial canvas,

I am ushered into the Presence of the Divine,

Awed at the glorious work of Your hand.

As I witness the infinite, glimmering pageant aloft,

I cannot help but proclaim as the Psalmist,

O LORD, how is it You are mindful of me?

Your handiwork, it steals my breath away!

As I gaze at the silky vastness above,

Insignificance threatens to overwhelm me.

But then I sense Your Spirit hovering near--

And I am immersed in inexplicable joy.

O LORD, whisper my name in the stillness.

Embrace me 'neath the velvety expanse.

Oh that I could linger here forever,

Softly enveloped in the peace of Your Presence.

Gaze

"...I come to you in the name of the Lord of Heaven's Armies—

The God of the armies of Israel, whom you have defied.

Today the Lord will conquer you..."

1 Samuel 17:45

"Who is this man?" they asked.

"Even the winds and waves obey him!"

Matthew 8:27b

"So humble yourselves before God.

Resist the devil, and he will flee from you."

James 4:7

"I know the LORD is always with me.

I will not be shaken, for He is right beside me."

Psalm 16:8

Melissa "Missy" Bishop

Fill my gaze, Lord, when giants are stalking,

And darkness is falling in the valley of fear.

Fill my gaze, Lord, when waves are crashing,

As the storm keeps raging all around.

Fill my gaze, Lord, when devils are threat'ning

Whispering their threats in the night.

For terror seeks to overtake me...

When the giant's vastness is what I see.

And currents pull me deeper and deeper...

When the waves' fierceness is what I see.

And foulness dripping with every lie...

When the devil's leering is what I see.

Fill my gaze, Lord, with Your Power--

Felling giants by Your name!

Fill my gaze, Lord, with Your Mercy--

Whispering Peace in the storm.

Fill my gaze, Lord, with Your Authority--

Scattering devils in Your path!

For every giant has to fall.

Every storm has to cease.

And the very devil has to flee--

By the Power of Your Name!

By the Mercy of Your Peace!

And by the Authority of the King of Kings!

Fill my gaze, Lord, with only You. Fill my gaze complete!

Heartbeats

"The Spirit and the bride say, "Come."

Let anyone who hears this say, "Come."

Let anyone who is thirsty come.

Let anyone who desires drink freely from the water of life…

He who is the faithful witness to all these things says,

"Yes, I am coming soon!"

Amen! Come, Lord Jesus!"

Revelation 22:17, 20

"You will show me the way of life,

Granting me the joy of your presence and

The pleasures of living with you forever."

Psalm 16:11

"And I will ask the Father, and He will give you another Advocate,

who will never leave you."

John 14:16

Heartbeats spent in Your Presence;

Mere droplets in an ocean of blue.

The kiss of Your Spirit so sweet

Leaves me longing for more of You.

I want to drown in Your Presence;

And long to see Your becoming face.

Quench my thirst for more of You--

Moments here are but a foretaste.

My spirit longs for Your Presence,

To kneel and worship before Your throne;

And to experience Your unveiled Glory--

Eternity spent in my heavenly home.

To join the angels in unhindered worship

Holy, Holy, Holy is Your name!

Just to be with Christ, my Savior

Even so, come Lord Jesus, come!

Selah

"O Lord, our Lord, your majestic name fills the earth!

Your glory is higher than the heavens."

Psalm 8:1

"But as for me, I will sing about your power.

Each morning I will sing with joy about your unfailing love.

For you have been my refuge, a place of safety when I am in distress."

Psalm 59:16

"Everything on earth will worship you;

They will sing your praises,

Shouting your name in glorious songs."

Psalm 66:4

"Then I will praise God's name with singing,

and I will honor Him with thanksgiving."

Psalm 69:30

Melissa "Missy" Bishop

I will sing to Your Name in the morning,

That time with You so sweet.

I will sing to Your Name at eventide,

Be near me, always, I breathe.

Pour Your melody into my heart,

A reflection of Your Light.

Whisper my name in the stillness,

Empower me with Your might.

I bring to You a sacrifice of praise,

Lifting up hands to Your name.

In the midst of turmoil and strife,

I will choose You, Lord, always.

Sometimes my prayer is hushed,

But Your Spirit sings through me.

In Christ Alone, my Cornerstone,

This hymn, sometimes I sing.

At times I long to be held so dear,

And lay my head on Your chest.

To breathe You in, this love so deep,

Wrapped in Your arms, and blessed.

Even on the battleground,

When the fighting is so fierce...

My eyes will look to You, O God,

And I will lift up my voice.

Through the times of testing,

When my faith is on the line;

Scarred and wounded from the battle,

Praise breaks the chains that bind.

Those times I do not understand,

Your plan, Your purpose in this fight.

I will still sing to You, my God,

This I will choose, every time.

For never once have You left me alone;

Neither valley nor mountain peak.

You are faithful, God, always faithful.

I sing, and celebrate the victory!   Selah

My Father's Eyes

"I pray that your hearts will be flooded with light

So that you can understand the confident hope He has given

To those He called—His holy people who are His rich and glorious inheritance."

Ephesians 1:18

"For the Lord God is our sun and shield.

He gives us grace and glory. The Lord will withhold no good thing

From those who do what is right.

O Lord of Heaven's Armies, what joy for those who trust in You."

Psalm 84:11-12

Echoes of Grace

O Lord of Angel armies

My soul delights in You alone.

Your unfailing love exceeds the heavenly heights.

For Your love endures forever

Your salvation knows no bounds.

The steps of the faithful You will light.

Throughout the span of time

And imaginations supreme

None other can compare to You.

For Your mercy is everlasting

And Your righteousness remains

To those who call You Faithful and True.

So that I might be called Your own

Your sacrifice knew no limit;

Love unfathomable You poured down.

My flesh indeed may falter

But Your hand of victory sustains me

You alone are my strong tower.

Helpless I must come

And surrender my life to You.

But my Father's eyes are never concealed.

O Lord, flood my heart with light--

The light of confident hope.

O Lord my God, You alone are my sun and shield.

Dawn of Grace

"O God, you are my God; I earnestly search for you.

My soul thirsts for you; my whole body longs for you in this parched and weary land where there is no water."

Psalm 63:1

"I long, yes, I faint with longing to enter the courts of the Lord.

With my whole being, body and soul,

I will shout joyfully to the living God."

Psalm 84:2

"So let us come boldly to the throne of our gracious God.

There we will receive his mercy, and we will find grace to help us when we need it most."

Hebrews 4:16

"The faithful love of the LORD never ends! His mercies never cease. Great is His faithfulness;

His mercies begin afresh each morning."

Lamentations 3:22-23

Melissa "Missy" Bishop

I wake with silent anticipation

New mercy floods the depths of my soul.

Eagerly I await the sound of Your voice.

Humbly awed by immeasurable favor.

The dawn of Your grace lights the sky.

As I come to the secret place.

I desire to be in Your Presence Lord

Imploring, show me the path to take.

My spirit feels heavy within me

In Your presence I am undone.

And with the depths of my entire being

I stand in awe before Your throne.

Enlighten the way before me, O God

With Your mercy, Your grace, profound

This ache I have, only You can fill

As I seek to follow the road ahead.

Immerse me in the pure anointing.

Use me Lord, as a beacon of hope

Your Spirit is calling me deeper still.

That others be drawn to Your embrace.

Lifeline

"Yes, I am the gate. Those who come in through me will be saved.

They will come and go freely and will find good pastures.

The thief's purpose is to steal and kill and destroy.

My purpose is to give them a rich and satisfying life."

John 10:9-10

"The Spirit of the Lord is upon me,

For he has anointed me to bring Good News to the poor.

He has sent me to proclaim that captives will be released,

That the blind will see,

That the oppressed will be set free,

And that the time of the Lord's favor has come."

Luke 4:18-19

Wandering through this sea of faces

I am struck to the depths of my heart.

For I see them as You reveal to me

Slowly drowning, and they fathom it not.

The enemy's lies have them blinded,

No light of life is in their eyes

Lives desperate for the love of the Savior

Lord, pierce their darkness with Your light.

This image of the lost and dying

Burns vivid in the recesses of my mind.

As the swirling eddy drags them deeper still—

How they need the Hope of mankind!

O Lord, pour Your words into my mouth,

And grant me those moments in time

That I may be Your hands and feet,

Offering Your blood stained lifeline.

Wanderer

"So he returned home to his father.

And while he was still a long way off, his father saw him coming.

Filled with love and compassion, he ran to his son, embraced him, and kissed him."

Luke 15:20

"For God loved the world so much that he gave his one and only Son, so that everyone who believes in him will not perish but have eternal life."

John 3:16

Melissa "Missy" Bishop

Wanderer, come just as you are;

The arms of the Lord are beckoning...

He knows the longing you cannot slake;

The lost look in your eyes He sees.

And He offers unmerited favor,

Forgiveness through faith is yours.

As the father who ran at the prodigal's return,

So Gods arms are spread open wide.

And though the road oft times is twisted,

His voice keeps calling your name.

The emptiness inside you've longed to fill;

The hopelessness that weighs you down—

Those are not the Father's will for you,

That is why He sent down His Son.

Regret has dragged you through the mire,

The way ahead in shadow is cloaked.

But the light of forgiveness and grace,

Through the Son's sacrifice He will bestow.

Wanderer, come just as you are;

The arms of the Lord are welcoming.

His heart is that you may know peace,

Accepting the gift so costly given.

All you need do is humbly ask,

Accepting what's already complete.

Then the void in your heart He'll fill with love,

And the angels in heaven will sing!

Wanderer, come just as you are...

The arms of the Lord are beckoning.

Rescue

"For 'Everyone who calls on the name of the Lord will be saved'".

Romans 10:13

"For everyone has sinned; we all fall short of God's glorious standard.

Yet God, with undeserved kindness, declares that we are righteous.

He did this through Christ Jesus when he freed us from the penalty for our sins."

Romans 3:23-24

"Jesus told him, 'I am the way, the truth, and the life.

No one can come to the Father, except through Me."

John 14:6

Melissa "Missy" Bishop

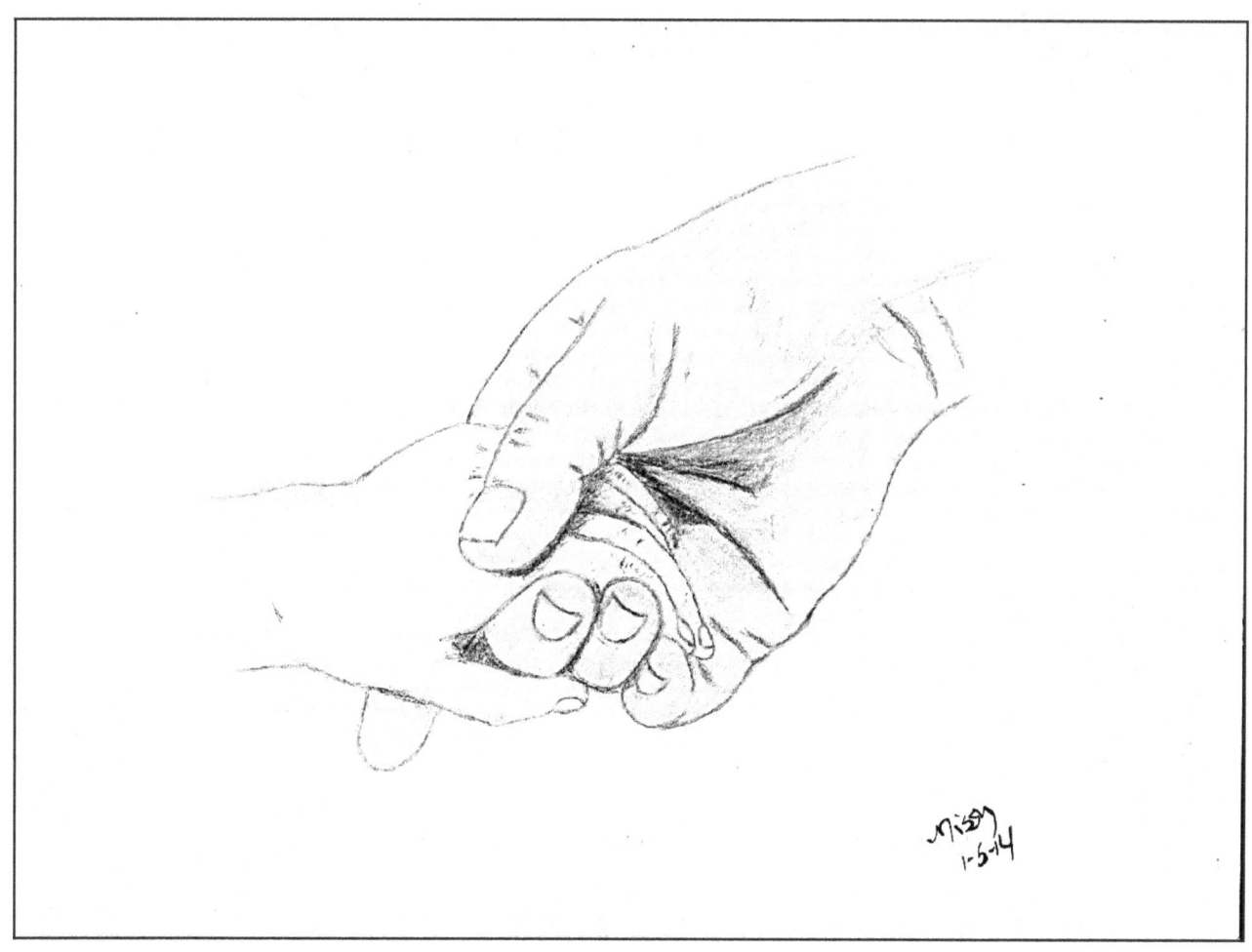

Tears streaming silently down my face;

Evidence of a pain held deep.

The chasm in my heart so empty;

A sense of brokenness complete.

You proved my worth with Calvary's blood

And Your unfailing love still waits.

Sweet glow of mercy pouring down

You whisper--My child, why hesitate?

Trying to fix myself on my own,

Only failing with each attempt.

Finally broken in surrender,

To You my burdened soul went.

Instantly to me Your hand reached down,

Offering such Amazing Grace.

The heavy chains of captivity severed

Like spider's silk by Your name.

The burdens I've carried far too long

Finally lifted off my frame.

You've been pursuing my heart entire

Waiting for the whisper of Your name.

Now the chasm of my heart

Filled complete with Love Divine.

You are the God of my salvation

Jesus, my Savior is mine!

Shinsei

"Show me the right path, O Lord; point out the road for me to follow.

Lead me by your truth and teach me, for you are the God who saves me.

All day long I put my hope in you."

Psalm 25:4-5

"And yet, O Lord, you are our Father.

We are the clay, and you are the potter.

We all are formed by your hand."

Isaiah 64:8

There is much I do not know;

But Your face, Lord, I will seek.

Grant me wisdom, mercy and courage;

Calm my struggles and my fears.

Take my failures and my strengths,

And shape me with Your love.

Jesus, hear my plea!

Breathe afresh on me Your Spirit.

My prayer, Mighty God, is this—

That you will lead me on the path ahead.

And guide me in the way everlasting—

This Way that is Holy and True.

For You alone are the Potter;

And I am only clay.

Mold me in Your image, Lord.

Little souls are watching—

Abba, help me to Teach them well.

Reflect Your eyes through me.

Warrior

"Pray in the Spirit at all times and on every occasion.

Stay alert and be persistent in your prayers for all believers everywhere."

Ephesians 6:18

"So we have not stopped praying for you since we first heard about you.

We ask God to give you complete knowledge of his will and

To give you spiritual wisdom and understanding.

Then the way you live will always honor and please the Lord,

And your lives will produce every kind of good fruit.

All the while, you will grow as you learn to know God better and better.

We also pray that you will be strengthened with all his

Glorious power so you will have all the endurance

and patience you need. May you be filled with joy, always thanking the Father.

He has enabled you to share in the inheritance

That belongs to his people, who live in the light."

Colossians 1:9-12

Melissa "Missy" Bishop

Bone weary from the fighting
Wounded and nearly spent.
And still the battle is raging
The armor you wear--RENT!

In the sights of the enemy
Days and months unremitting.
Mounting despair pins you down;
Breathless--the death blow--FALLING!

God knows you are exhausted.
And giving up may promise ease.
But the enemy is whispering lies;
He knows not but to deceive.

Fear not, fellow soldier.
Don't give in! Hold your ground.
Endure but a little while longer.
I'll fight for you, head bowed down.

On my knees I will go to battle.
Praying by the Spirit's might!
Arms upraised to the LORD of Hosts;
This final hour, will turn the tide.

Treasure

"This is my commandment:

Love each other in the same way I have loved you.

There is no greater love than to lay down one's life for one's friends."

John 15:12-13

"Timely advice is lovely, like golden apples in a silver basket."

Proverbs 25:11

"A friend is always loyal, and a brother is born to help in time of need."

Proverbs 17:17

Echoes of Grace

Melissa "Missy" Bishop

Where do I find the words

When words cannot describe

The essence of a friendship

And its value in my life?

Bonds made not by human hands,

But sent from the Father of lights.

Both as strong as a tree in a hurricane,

And as gentle as a starry night.

Sometimes that quiet understanding,

Simply providing a listening ear;

And strength to share the burden,

To quietly hold me near.

Other times a word fitly spoken,

Offering healing for unseen scars;

The balm of promise and love,

Reflections from a sincere heart.

Where do I find the words?

How I wish I could express!

The essence of your friendship

It's a treasure—I am blessed.

A Mother's Prayers

"Accept my prayer as incense offered to you,

And my upraised hands as an evening offering."

Psalm 141:2

"And when he took the scroll, the four living beings and the twenty-four elders

Fell down before the Lamb.

Each one had a harp,

And they held gold bowls filled with incense,

Which are the prayers of God's people."

Revelation 5:8

"Charm is deceptive,

And beauty does not last;

But a woman who fears the LORD

Will be greatly praised."

Proverbs 31:30

Melissa "Missy" Bishop

Many times in the still of night,

A mother gently kneels.

And every burden held in her heart,

She pours out to You through tears.

When a seed's been newly planted,

In the shelter of her womb,

She asks of You for wisdom,

And for Your Grace on her unborn.

Through sleepless nights in shadows,

When she cradles, comforts, cares.

She prays for strength and whispers

Sweet lullabies through weary tears.

Through first words, first steps,

And through the terrible twos

She whispers prayers to You each day

And prays for Grace to make it through.

Each new day of school,

As the seasons come and go

She prays Your hand of protection

And angels to guard them so.

When their days of childhood are past

And the roads of life diverge,

She casts them gently into Your care

But remembers the years they were hers.

And when she's passed beyond this life

Into the glorious one beyond,

Those faithful prayers, through all the years,

Arise like incense before Your throne.

A mother's prayers, it's often said,

Are as close in this life to be,

A reflection of God's own love

And for her children, a legacy.

For the Love of a Child

"Children are a gift from the Lord; they are a reward from him.

Children born to a young man are like arrows in a warrior's hands.

How joyful is the man whose quiver is full of them!"

Psalm 127:3-5a

"You made all the delicate, inner parts of my body

And knit me together in my mother's womb.

Thank you for making me so wonderfully complex!

Your workmanship is marvelous—how well I know it.

You watched me as I was being formed in utter seclusion,

As I was woven together in the dark of the womb.

You saw me before I was born.

Every day of my life was recorded in your book

Every moment was laid out before a single day had passed."

Psalm 139:13-16

Melissa "Missy" Bishop

A tiny hand reaching forth,

To grasp onto yours tight.

A rosebud mouth to smile,

To giggle in sheer delight.

Large eyes fringed with thick lashes,

To gaze at you, filled with love.

A child is a gift to you,

Sent down from Heaven above.

The joy of having such a treasure--

To hold, to cherish, to give.

For the love of a child

Is reason enough to live.

The Sweet Sound of Silence

"But Jesus often withdrew to the wilderness for prayer."

Luke 5:16

"Go out and stand before me on the mountain," the Lord told him.

And as Elijah stood there, the Lord passed by,

And a mighty windstorm hit the mountain.

It was such a terrible blast that the rocks were torn loose,

But the Lord was not in the wind.

After the wind there was an earthquake,

But the Lord was not in the earthquake.

And after the earthquake there was a fire,

But the Lord was not in the fire.

And after the fire there was the sound of a gentle whisper.

When Elijah heard it, he wrapped his face in his cloak

And went out and stood at the entrance of the cave.

And a voice said, "What are you doing here, Elijah?"

1 Kings 19:11-13

Many sounds assault our ears,

As we go from day to day.

Some are loud, others soft,

And some in between.

There may be booming thunder

Shaking the earth!

Or maybe the gentle pitter pat

Of raindrops on a window pane.

Wind whispering through trees,

Gently rustling branches.

Or the screaming of crowded streets,

Making us want to cover our ears!

The gurgling of a stream

Deep in the mountain forest.

The roar of a mighty waterfall.

The list could go on.

Though sound is a wonder,

And there are many good things to hear--

Sometimes the best sound in the world,

Is the sweet sound of silence.

For only in the quietness

Is it possible to attune

To the still small voice of God,

A gentle whisper calling us home.

He Came

"Look! The virgin will conceive a child!

She will give birth to a son,

And they will call him Immanuel,

Which means 'God is with us.'"

Matthew 1:23

"But the time is coming—indeed it's here now—

When true worshipers will worship the Father

In spirit and in truth.

The Father is looking for those who

Will worship him that way.

For God is Spirit, so those who worship him

Must worship in spirit and in truth."

John 4:23-24

"Glory to God in the highest heaven,

And peace on earth to those with whom

God is pleased."

Luke 2:14

Melissa "Missy" Bishop

He came for shepherds abiding,

Guarding their flocks by night.

The angels heralding in the sky,

The birth of the Savior is nigh!

He came for wise men seeking,

Following the star so bright.

Bowing before their Messiah King,

And offering gifts so prized.

He came wrapped in humanity,

Because of His love so vast.

Choosing to leave the splendor of Heaven,

To dwell among the least of us.

He came to live a life so pure,

Then willingly to lay it down.

Born to seek and save the lost,

To bridge the gap that was torn.

He came for any and all,

Who with childlike faith stand fast--

And search for Him with all their heart

Ever abiding in 'God with Us'.

Hero

"He was oppressed and treated harshly yet he never said a word.

He was led like a lamb to the slaughter.

And as a sheep is silent before the shearers,

He did not open his mouth."

Isaiah 53:7

"And now you Gentiles have also heard the truth,

The Good News that God saves you.

And when you believed in Christ,

He identified you as his own by giving you

The Holy Spirit, whom he promised long ago."

Ephesians 1:13

"He is so rich in kindness and grace that He purchased our freedom with the blood of

His Son and forgave our sins."

Ephesians 1:7

> Note: The bracelet referred to in this poem is one I wore while serving in the Air Force. Bracelets such as mine were worn by many service men and women to honor the memories of our fellow soldiers who were killed or missing in action in years past.

Melissa "Missy" Bishop

I never knew Everett Kerr,

Although his bracelet I wear.

I know but a few simple facts,

From the inscription it bears

Disappeared in Laos,

1966 was the year.

That's all I know of your fate,

Air Force Colonel and Mountaineer.

Your bravery, courage and sacrifice,

Of this I know for sure.

Who you left behind?

I wish I knew more.

You are only one of many,

Soldiers far and near.

Who paid the ultimate sacrifice

For those you held dear.

So many have given their lives,

So that we can remain free

I salute you all,

For the sacrifice made for me.

Melissa "Missy" Bishop

But another made that sacrifice;

And Him, I do know well.

For He bore my sins upon a tree;

And rescued my soul from hell.

Willingly He was led;

And willingly He died;

His blood bought freedom for all;

His resurrection, eternal life.

I haven't met Him face to face;

Though one sweet day I will.

But His word is hidden in my heart;

His Spirit is my seal.

Jesus Christ, Son of God;

Savior, Rescuer, Friend.

Thank You for Your sacrifice!

Redeeming the soul of man!

Grace and Truth

"So if the Son sets you free, you are truly free."

John 8:36

"So the Word became human and made his home among us.

He was full of unfailing love and faithfulness.

And we have seen his glory, the glory of the Father's one and only Son."

John 1:14

"The light shines in the darkness, and the darkness can never extinguish it."

John 1:5

Echoes of Grace

Melissa "Missy" Bishop

Why was it You came,

So full of Grace and Truth--

Knowing what You'd face,

Leaving Heaven to come to earth?

Why did You set aside Your glory

Allowing us to catch a glimpse--

Seeing we are but sinful creatures?

It's more than I can comprehend!

The Grace You extend so willingly,

Astounding, for one and all!

Was by Your blood, shed drop by drop,

Available for those who call.

And it's by Your Truth alone

That prisoners can walk away--

For no chain is strong enough to hold

Those loosened in Jesus' Name.

So You came to be Light in the darkness,

That the sinner might understand--

You came to shine with brightness;

The glory of God in Your countenance.

Whatever this life on earth bestows,

You offer a beautiful hope,

A future with You eternal--

And to the enduring these words, Well Done!

Glimpses of Glory (You Are Near)

"For in him we live and move and exist."

Acts 17:28a

"My dove is hiding behind the rocks, behind an outcrop on the cliff.

Let me see your face; let me hear your voice.

For your voice is pleasant, and your face is lovely."

Song of Solomon 2:14

"O LORD, our Lord, Your majestic name fills the earth!

Your glory is higher than the heavens."

Psalm 8:1

Glimpses of glory are all around,

Displays of Your handiwork steal my breath away.

All Creation calls out Your name,

And I know that You are near.

When sunlight pierces the cloak of rain,

Eagerly for rainbows I search the skies.

And in the inky black veil of night

O to chance a falling star!

Within the myriad array of each new dawn,

And at days' end when darkness claims the light--

I see Your glory there on display,

And I feel wrapped in Your arms of love.

How could I not see Your handprint

On the vast canvas stretched above?

When I nearly burst in awe at Your splendor;

The heavens painted by Your Master hand.

O Lord, help me to glimpse Your amazing glory

As I live, move and breathe in You.

Even in moments of mere simplicity,

To expect Your Presence made known.

I long to live in breathless abandon,

With senses tuned to Your holy timbre--

As You romance my heart with moments of glory,

And reveal how close You are.

Almost

"He gave his life to free us from every kind of sin,

To cleanse us, and to make us his very own people,

Totally committed to doing good deeds."

Titus 2:14

"We know what real love is because Jesus gave up his life for us."

1 Peter 3:16a

"And may you have the power to understand,

As all God's people should, how wide, how long, how high,

And how deep his love is.

May you experience the love of Christ,

Though it is too great to understand fully.

Then you will be made complete with all the fullness of life

And power that comes from God."

Ephesians 3:18-19

Melissa "Missy" Bishop

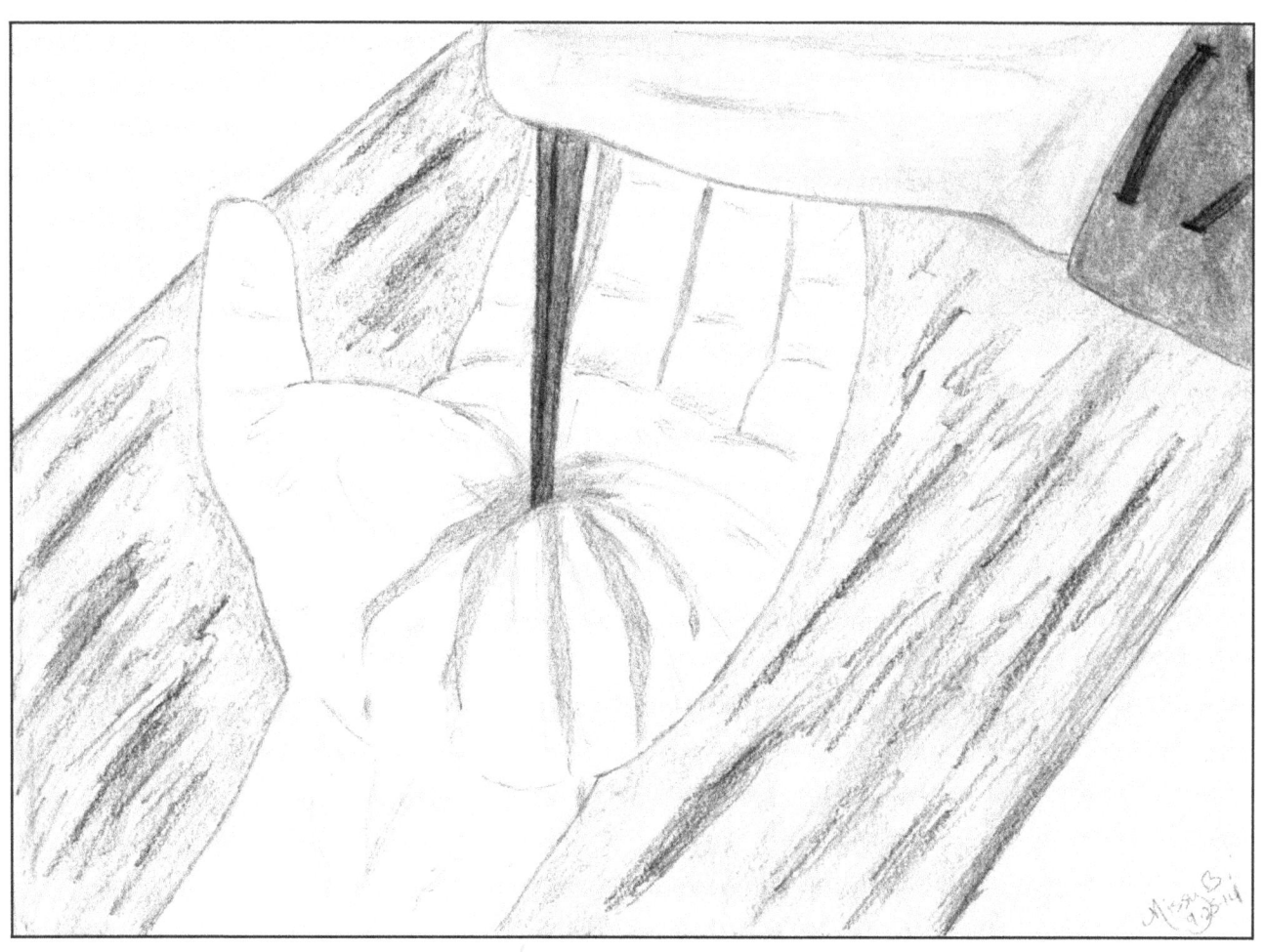

Almost can I imagine the gruesome scene that day;

Your body bruised and broken, lifted high for all to see.

And almost can I hear the hammer striking again and again.

Driving the nails that pierced Your flesh, and bound You to that tree.

Almost can I hear You say, 'Father, please forgive';

As soldiers gambled 'neath Your feet and passersby mocked and jeered.

And almost can I hear the gasping thief: 'Remember me this day'

As he surrendered his spirit to Your embrace; and so believed.

Echoes of Grace

Almost can I see Mary, her face worn with grief;

As she beheld her Son and Savior, body wracked with pain.

And almost can I see heaven darkened by the grief of a holy God,

As the Father turned His eyes from His one and only Son.

Almost can I hear You cry: 'My God, why have You forsaken Me'?

As the weight of humanity's sin heaped upon Your sinless being.

And almost can I hear through Your parched lips, 'I thirst';

A request for water, to fulfill--and to sooth Your weariness.

Almost can I hear the finality in Your voice,

As You completed the task and cried "It is Finished!"

And almost can I hear with Your final breath

As You committed Your spirit to the Father's care.

Almost can I imagine the ground shaking and lightening flashing,

As the mighty temple veil was ripped by God's great hand!

And almost can I hear the centurion's cry of amazement,

As he realized at that moment who it was he beheld.

Almost can I imagine the sword that pierced Your side,

And the blood and water that flowed from Your still form.

And almost can I picture them lowering Your body down,

Then carrying You, tenderly, to a borrowed tomb.

But...almost, can I fathom the depth of a love so great,

That caused You so to suffer and to die in such agony?

And...almost can I understand the sacrifice made on my behalf;

To restore the broken relationship between God and humanity?

No! Almost doesn't come close or can it ever attain;

For the magnitude of my Savior's love that held You to that tree!

And almost cannot dare to illustrate nor describe

The depth of my gratitude and awe for my Savior's love for me!

It is Finished!

"When Jesus had tasted it, he said, "It is finished!"

Then he bowed his head and released his spirit."

John 19:30

"I am the living one. I died, but look—

I am alive forever and ever!

And I hold the keys of death and the grave."

Revelation 1:18

"The next day John saw Jesus coming toward him and said,

"Look! The Lamb of God who takes away the sin of the world!"

John 1:29

Melissa "Missy" Bishop

It is finished!

Your sacrifice complete.

With those words

You covered every need.

You, the Lamb with no blemish,

God clothed in humanity.

The crimson tide that flowed

To save a wretch like me.

What amazing Love and Grace

That led You to that hill--

To face the nails, the crown, the spear

To take on Yourself our guilt.

King of Glory, Behold the Lamb!

Hanging there, love pouring down.

Gazing before, You saw each of us

And chose the shame, the pain.

Death, hell, and the grave

And all our sins you claimed--

Healing for every sickness

That day, You overcame!

It is finished!

When You breathed Your last,

Everything was complete

Present, future, and past.

So for every trial, every test

The victory's already won!

For when You said It is Finished!

The work, forever, was done.

Valley

"Even when I walk through the darkest valley,

I will not be afraid, for you are close beside me."

Psalm 23:4a

"And now, dear brothers and sisters, one final thing.

Fix your thoughts on what is true, and honorable, and right,

And pure, and lovely, and admirable.

Think about things that are excellent and worthy of praise.

Keep putting into practice all you learned and received from me—

Everything you heard from me and saw me doing.

Then the God of peace will be with you."

Philippians 4:8-9

Melissa "Missy" Bishop

Walking through this valley

Never felt so alone.

Days stretched to months

Will sunshine touch my face again?

Believing Your promises are true

Like dearly loved, never forsaken, always near.

But filled with feelings so deceitful

Not needed, unlovely, forgotten.

Cannot stop their tirade.

You alone can fill this void.

But where are You, Lord?

Your voice seems silent in this darkness

No sentiment pierces through.

Still holding a thread of hope

This fog will rise from my soul.

And Your whisper will reach my ears

As I fall in Your embrace.

Healing

"To all who mourn in Israel,

He will give a crown of beauty for ashes,

A joyous blessing instead of mourning

Festive praise instead of despair.

In their righteousness, they will be like great oaks

That the Lord has planted for his own glory."

Isaiah 61:3

"Then Jesus said, "Come to me,

All of you who are weary and carry heavy burdens,

And I will give you rest."

Matthew 11:28

"I have not stopped thanking God for you.

I pray for you constantly."

Ephesians 1:16

Echoes of Grace

Pain, like a thorn, pierces my soul in the night;

Sorrow upon sorrow, rages as a storm tossed sea.

Hold my hand lest I drown in this blackness;

Be near me as I grasp for the Light.

Walk with me, though the way is dark and dreary;

Stay with me, lest this darkness overwhelm.

I cannot make it on my own.

I am weak. I will falter.

Yet I know that I am not alone.

There in the distance, What is it I see?

The dawn of His salvation, shining on the horizon,

Healing, riding on His wings.

The darkness is losing its power.

It cannot hold back the Light.

His promise--to make beauty from the ashes,

And to straighten the way before.

Walk with me, my Friend,

With Him, the cord is strong.

Let us continue together,

Through the garden of His mercy and love.

It is a sweet rose blossoming;

Fragrant with everlasting grace.

Scars

"So be truly glad. There is wonderful joy ahead,

Even though you have to endure many trials for a little while.

These trials will show that your faith is genuine.

It is being tested as fire tests and purifies gold—

Though your faith is far more precious than mere gold.

So when your faith remains strong through many trials,

It will bring you much praise and glory and honor

On the day when Jesus Christ is revealed

To the whole world."

1 Peter 1:6-7

"And we know that God causes everything to work

Together for the good of those who love God

And are called according to his purpose for them."

Romans 8:28

Melissa "Missy" Bishop

Wounds still fresh from the battle,

Scars soon to take their place.

My faith's been on the firing line,

But still... I know there's Grace.

My questions abound in these flames,

Asking what lesson is there here?

But my hope remains in You, O God,

In these trials, relentless and fierce.

The promises I know are true,

Remind me: You always hear--

Every whispered prayer...every sorrow.

You've captured each silent tear.

In You there's beauty from these ashes,

And gold, by fire, made pure.

Please use this pain I have suffered,

To help a child of Yours stand firm.

Hope

"Therefore, since we are surrounded by such a huge crowd

Of witnesses to the life of faith, let us strip off every weight

That slows us down, especially the sin that so easily trips us up.

And let us run with endurance the race God has set before us.

We do this by keeping our eyes on Jesus,

The champion who initiates and perfects our faith.

Because of the joy awaiting him,

He endured the cross, disregarding its shame.

Now he is seated in the place of honor

Beside God's throne."

Hebrews 12:1-2

"At about three o 'clock, Jesus called out with a loud voice,

'Eli, Eli, lema sabachthani?', which means,

'My God, My God, why have You abandoned Me?'"

Matthew 27:46

The road's been long and arduous

Through valleys dim with despair.

Solitude has been my cloak--

But no sanctuary is found there.

Through countless months of plodding

And seeking to escape this mire--

At times I've begun to question

My hope hanging on the wire.

Feeling so alone in the struggle

Even falling for the enemy's lies

Why can't I get the answers?

Why do You seem so silent?

But I've come too far in the faith

To let go of Your hand

And even when You seem distant

I know You're there--You understand.

For even You have felt abandoned

When on that dark and lonely hill

You took all my failures and mistakes—

Yes, You know just how I feel.

So I will keep on trusting

Still hoping, believing in You.

No matter what happens in the fire

My faith will see me through.

Undone

"Then I said, "It's all over! I am doomed, for I am a sinful man.

I have filthy lips, and I live among a people with filthy lips.

Yet I have seen the King, the Lord of Heaven's Armies...'

Then I heard the Lord asking, "Whom should I send as a

Messenger to this people? Who will go for us?"

I said, "Here I am. Send me."

Isaiah 6:5,8

"With his own blood—not the blood of goats and calves—

He entered the Most Holy Place once for all time

and secured our redemption forever."

Hebrews 9:12

"These were His instructions to them:

The harvest is great, but the workers are few.

So pray to the Lord who is in charge of the harvest;

Ask Him to send more workers into His fields."

Luke 10:2

Melissa "Missy" Bishop

What expression can describe the perfection of Holiness

That Isaiah experienced the year Uzziah passed?

Mere human observations are deficient

To capture and pen a revelation so vast.

The burning ones praising in reverential awe,

With silken wings cascading as they hovered.

Calling Holy, Holy, Holy together as one,

To the Lord of Heaven's Armies, forever enthroned.

The earthquake resounding with their utterance,

As the smoke of glory encompassed the room.

Purest of Light—a burning flame!

My Lord and my God! I too am undone!

Just as Isaiah cried 'Woe is me!'

As Your holy Presence permeated his heart—

So my own soul cries in awe and wonder;

My inmost thoughts and whims made stark.

But purity was bestowed with a fiery coal

Upon the penitent prophet's lips;

As he offered his life in humble service

So a hard-hearted people might repent.

Forgiveness for me was bought once and for all,

When the veil of separation was rent.

Granted completely by the Lamb who was slain,

And crimson blood washed clean my heart.

I cry out with Isaiah when asked 'Who will go?'

To share this Word of Life proffered?

Lord, here I am—send me!

Ignited by Your Spirit—I am Yours.

All Things New

"This means that anyone who belongs to

Christ has become a new person.

The old life is gone; a new life has begun!"

2 Corinthians 5:17

"So be strong and courageous!

Do not be afraid and do not panic before them.

For the Lord your God will personally go ahead of you.

He will neither fail you nor abandon you."

Deuteronomy 31:6

"The way of the righteous is like the first gleam of dawn,

Which shines ever brighter until the full light of day."

Proverbs 4:18

Melissa "Missy" Bishop

Looking back at the path I've trodden

Through days and months long past;

The scales on my eyes have fallen away

And I see where Your hand was steadfast.

All through that darkest valley

And the storms that raged with no relief;

You still were my strong tower

Even when my humanity brought disbelief.

Those battles that tried to destroy my faith

And cause me to doubt Your truth;

I know now they made me stronger

My faith was tried—but it made it through.

So today I breathe my prayer of thanks

For Your faithfulness steadfast and sure;

Through the fires of trouble and tribulation

Your mercy makes all things new.

Above the Waves

"And I am certain that God, who began the good work within you,

Will continue his work until it is finally finished

On the day when Christ Jesus returns."

Philippians 1:6

"But you are not like that, for you are a chosen people.

You are royal priests, a holy nation,

God's very own possession.

As a result, you can show others the goodness of God,

For he called you out of the darkness

Into his wonderful light."

1 Peter 2:9

"I did this so you would trust not in human wisdom

But in the power of God."

1 Corinthians 2:5

You called me out of darkness

Offering freedom from the chains that bind.

So why do I still fight these battles,

Succumbing again to the torture in my mind?

At times my faith is stronger than fear,

And like Peter, I step into the unknown.

But all too often my eyes fall away—

Forgive me Lord! That's not the way You've shown.

Why can't I walk in the freedom You've purchased

Melissa "Missy" Bishop

Instead of reclaiming the chains of the past?

For those You free are freed forever—

And those shackles are severed by forgiveness.

Through wars waged and battles fought,

Scars have shaped who I've become.

But in You I am a new creation—

You promise to complete the work begun.

You continually call me by name—

Inviting me to dance upon the waves;

To be a child of the Most High God,

Saturated with peace and grace.

Your ways and thoughts are higher

Than I can ever comprehend.

And You offer life so abundant

To everyone who calls on Your name.

When my gaze falters, as it surely shall,

And I start to sink in the storm—

I will call upon my Savior true:

Your faithfulness has never let me down.

Spirit, lead me deeper and deeper.

Allow Your light to shine through.

I long for more of Your might and power:

To be a vessel willingly used.

When my confidence is weak and faltering,

Lift me up above the waves.

That my faith will stand in Your power,

Sustained in Your mercy and grace.

My Prayer

"Take my yoke upon you. Let me teach you,

Because I am humble and gentle at heart,

And you will find rest for your souls.

For my yoke is easy to bear,

And the burden I give you is light."

Matthew 11:29-30

"So you have not received a spirit that makes you fearful slaves.

Instead, you received God's Spirit when he adopted you as his own children.

Now we call him, "Abba, Father."

Romans 8:15

O let me hear the whisper of my name

Drawing me close to Your side.

I long to be in Your divine presence;

For I know mercy there I'll find.

I need to feel Your tangible nearness,

Where Your Spirit and mine intertwine.

As a daddy who draws His daughter close;

Offering strength and promising 'All is fine'.

For no matter the heartache that's come my way

In my Father's embrace all is well.

You extend Your yoke to lighten mine,

For my Abba knows I am weak and frail.

You promise those who seek You in truth

Will find the One our hearts desire.

Lord, I long for Your sweet embrace;

Feeling Your heartbeat next to mine.

When I cannot find words to utter,

And I'm grasping at those fleeting thoughts;

Your embrace is what matters most to me--

'My child', You say, 'why fret'?

'Let go of the things that weigh you down,

Drawing strength from the One who's true.

You are a daughter of the Most High God.

I gave My Son for you.'

God, forgive me for my weakness;

For letting fear displace my faith.

Once again, let me hear You whisper,

Speaking my name, offering Grace.

Embrace

"Worship the Lord in all his holy splendor.

Let all the earth tremble before him."

Psalm 96:9

"Since we are receiving a Kingdom that is unshakable, let us be thankful and please

God by worshiping him with holy fear and awe.

For our God is a devouring fire."

Hebrews 12:28-29

The Lord replied to Moses, "I will indeed do what you have asked,

for I look favorably on you, and I know you by name."

Moses responded, "Then show me your glorious presence."

Exodus 33:17-18

When Your Presence lingers,

And I'm surrounded by Your glory,

I can only breathe You in

For You are life to me.

In the beauty of Your holiness,

When I can merely kneel,

The sweet glow of Your mercy,

Envelopes me--pulls me near.

All my cares--all my struggles,

They diminish in that place.

For when You draw me closer

What matters only is Your embrace.

You fill my being entire—

In You I am complete!

Breathe on me, Holy Spirit.

Immerse me in Your peace.

Peace

"Create in me a clean heart, O God.

Renew a loyal spirit within me."

Psalm 51:10

"Whatever is good and perfect comes down to us

From God our Father, who created all the

Lights in the heavens.

He never changes or casts a shifting shadow.

He chose to give birth to us by giving us

His true word. And we,

Out of all creation,

Became his prized possession."

James 1:17-18

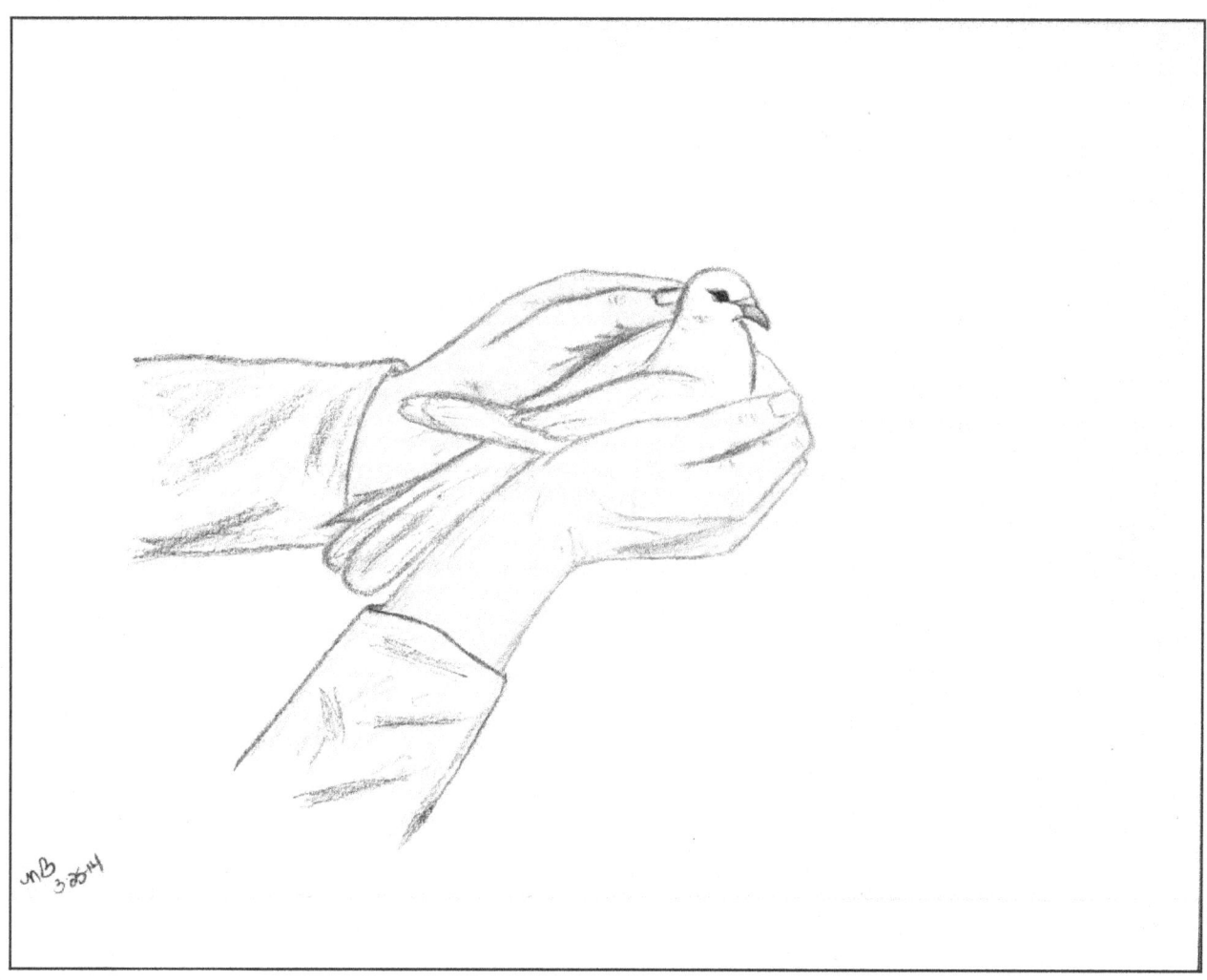

You've numbered my every heartbeat--

Each breath of life is in Your hands.

All that I am or ever will be

I owe to the Creator—Elohim.

Yet too often I take for granted

Every perfect gift poured down.

And I've wasted moments so precious--

Forgetting Your master plan.

For You came to give us life abundant--

Not fraught with heartache and despair.

Those moments spent in worry and trepidation

Steal the peace that You would share.

O Lord, quiet my clamorous anxieties

When they threaten to overwhelm.

So I can hear Your still small voice--

Whispering Peace in the midst of the storm.

And create a new heart within me;

One that only offers praise to Your name.

Anticipating the great things You have in store--

Instead of vain imaginings out of my hands.

For the One who painted the heavens;

And formed the earth at His command--

He holds my every moment

And has inscribed my name on His hand.

Tapestry

"Your own ears will hear Him.

Right behind you a voice will say,

"This is the way you should go,"

Whether to the right or to the left."

Isaiah 30:21

"The Lord directs the steps of the godly.

He delights in every detail of their lives."

Psalm 37:23

"For God knew His people in advance,

And He chose them to become like His Son,

So that His Son would be the firstborn

Among many brothers and sisters."

Romans 8:29

Gazing back at the story of my life,

Through adventures, heartaches, and growth—

The hand of my God has led me onward,

Grace chasing on His wings of love.

Long before I first called His Name,

And accepted the forgiveness bestowed--

God's plan divine was already in place,

His sovereign hand weaving, this I know.

After, with winding roads and open plains,

Across valleys and oceans blue--

His hand was creating a tapestry of Grace,

And His eyes were on me, through and through.

With many unknowns and ways unseen,

My steps already were made true—

And in this journey of invisible faith,

God's hand never once withdrew.

Yes, my life is a tapestry of Grace,

Set apart for the Master to use--

Leading me down the straight and narrow,

Designing a story of brilliant hues.

Dancing in the Light

"For the Lord your God is living among you.

He is a mighty savior. He will take delight in you with gladness.

With his love, he will calm all your fears.

He will rejoice over you with joyful songs."

Zephaniah 3:17

"The faithful love of the Lord never ends!

His mercies never cease.

Great is his faithfulness;

His mercies begin afresh each morning."

Lamentations 3:22-23

"I long for the LORD more than sentries long for the dawn,

Yes, more than sentries long for the dawn."

Psalm 130:6

Melissa "Missy" Bishop

Dancing in the Light of Your Presence

Fully surrendered to Your embrace.

You sing over me with gladness

And shower me with Your Grace.

In the fresh dew of the morning

Where Mercy is found anew;

I'm awed at the splendor of Your radiance--

The whisper of Love renewed.

The essence of holiness Divine

Envelopes me with Peace unexplained.

And as I breathe deeply of You

I'm attuned to the call of my name.

Gently warmed in the glow of Your Presence

As the dawn pierces darkest night;

Unmerited favor stirs the air around me

Joy, sweet joy, is mine!

So I dance in the Light of Your Presence

And surrender to Your embrace;

As You sing over me with gladness

And shower me with Your Grace.

Saturated with Grace

"Harmony is as refreshing as the dew from Mount Hermon

That falls on the mountains of Zion.

And there the LORD has pronounced His blessing,

Even life everlasting."

Psalm 133:3

"Let us, then, feel very sure that we can come before

God's throne where there is grace.

There we can receive mercy and grace

To help us when we need it."

Hebrews 4:16

"We have seen this hope as an anchor for the soul,

Sure and strong. It enters behind the curtain

In the Most Holy Place in heaven,

Where Jesus has gone ahead of us and for us."

Hebrews 6:19-20a

Echoes of Grace

Patiently there You were waiting

As I entered the secret place.

And there I was met with arms wide open

Drawing me tenderly to Your embrace.

Gently to Your shoulder I laid my head

As cords of love drew me close.

And together we walked in the early morning

Tears falling silently down my face.

The kiss of Your Presence so soft

Overwhelmed me with a love so true.

All I could fathom was Your nearness

Your Spirit surrounding, all I knew.

And then You invited me to dance

Your tender mercy holding me fast.

As all else faded into the gray,

Tears mingled with the dew of Grace.

No words there were to be spoken

As we danced in fellowship so sweet.

Harmony as refreshing as the dawn

And Grace saturating my wounded heart.

Two Hearts

"A person standing alone can be attacked and defeated,

But two can stand back-to-back and conquer.

Three are even better, for a triple-braided cord

Is not easily broken."

Ecclesiastes 4:12

"Three things will last forever—

Faith, hope, and love—

And the greatest of these is love."

1 Corinthians 13:13

Melissa "Missy" Bishop

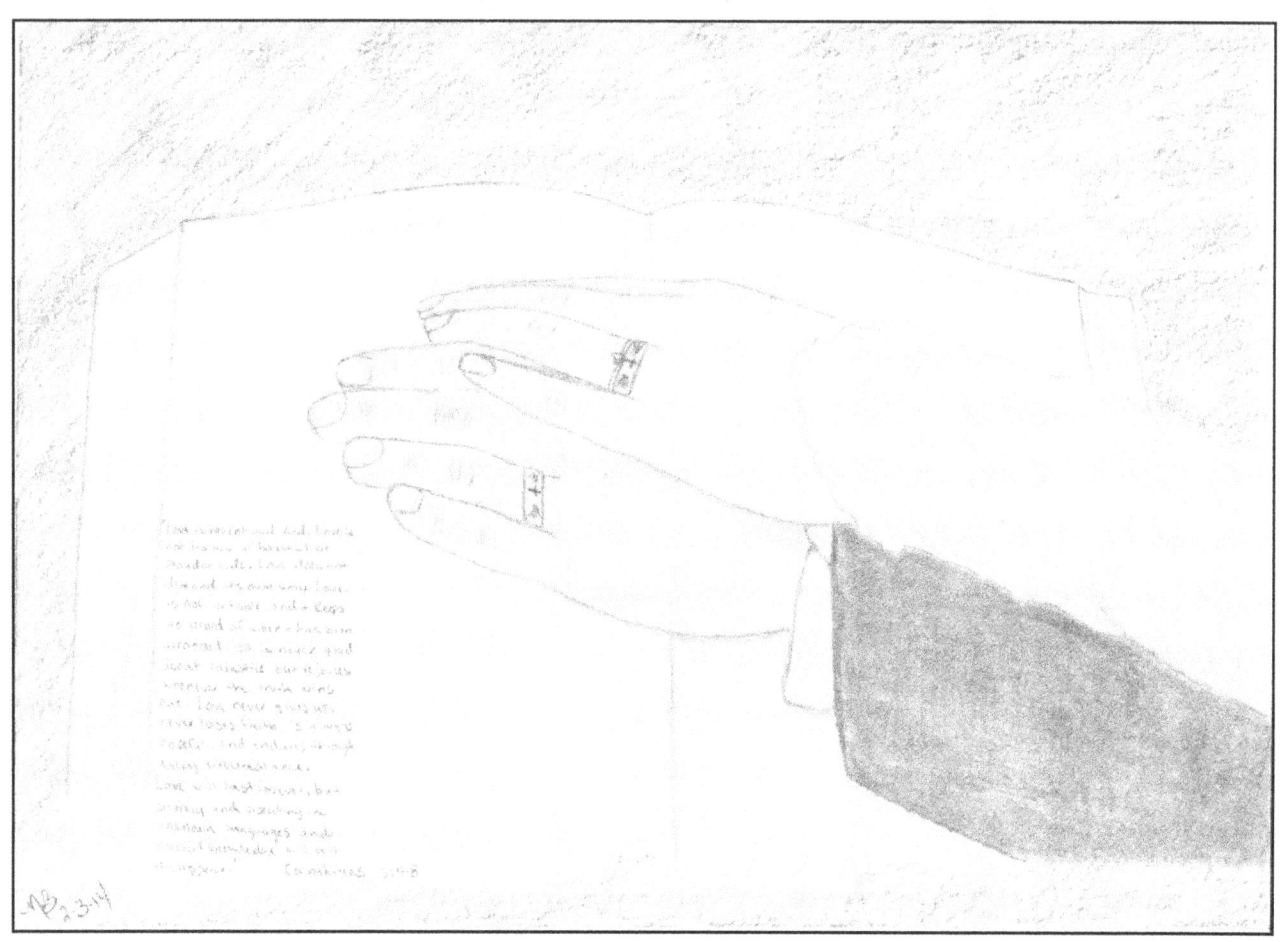

Two hearts joined by love Divine,

Created by the Master Himself.

Pledged to endure 'til Kingdom come.

To have and to hold at last.

Woman and man by the Spirit joined,

As God above ordained.

Two lives melded, completing the other,

Vows whispered, fingers entwined.

Two rings remain the symbol

Of vows this day exchanged;

And with Jesus--Redeemer, Friend,

The threefold cord remains.

Here you are, now husband and wife,

Together, forever, decreed;

A Love to last, by God above,

From this day to eternity.

I Love You More

"I am my beloved's, And my beloved is mine."

Song of Solomon 6:3

"Place me like a seal over your heart, like a seal on your arm.

For love is as strong as death, its jealousy as enduring as the grave.

Love flashes like fire, the brightest kind of flame."

Song of Solomon 8:6

"'This explains why a man leaves his father and mother and is joined to his wife,

and the two are united into one.' Since they are no longer two but one..."

Mark 10:7-8

Echoes of Grace

For my husband, Gary

I love you more at each day's end

Than the love each day before.

And more and more as time goes by,

I find ways to love you more.

From the first moment I saw you

And your eyes rose to mine,

The blossom of love began to grow;

Melissa "Missy" Bishop

Yes, I believe in love at first sight.

From the first time you held my hand,

And from your first tender kiss,

I knew my heart was yours forever,

I've loved you more ever since.

The day you asked if I'd be your bride;

A day emblazoned on my soul!

I thought then, How I love you!

But still, my love for you grows.

Many years have passed

Since the day our hearts entwined.

But my love for you diminishes not,

Thank the Lord in Heaven you are mine!

I'll love you my Dear,

'Til mountains crash into the sea.

I'll love you to the moon and back,

And on through eternity!

A Place That I Envision

"Then the Lord God planted a garden in Eden in the east,

And there he placed the man he had made…"

"A river flowed from the land of Eden,

Watering the garden and then dividing

Into four branches…"

"Then the Lord God said, "It is not good for the man

To be alone. I will make a

Helper who is just right for him.""

Genesis 2:8, 10, 18

"So God created human beings in his own image.

In the image of God he created them;

Male and female he created them."

Genesis 1:27

"God will do this, for he is faithful to do what he says,

And he has invited you into partnership

With his Son, Jesus Christ our Lord."

1 Corinthians 1:9

There is a place that I envision,

Somewhere in this land.

A place where I and the one I love,

Can walk together hand in hand.

There is a path that we can follow,

Meandering through the trees.

And trickling slowly by our side,

Is a shallow mountain stream.

The sunlight filters down upon us,

Through the broad overhanging leaves.

Leaving patchworks of light,

Dancing around as it pleases.

There will be no sound;

Except for that of the song bird's call.

And of course the gentle shuffling,

Of our slow, unrushed foot falls.

This scene I see is perfect!

As perfect as can be.

And the love that we share,

Shall last for all eternity!

Come Away

"If you look for me wholeheartedly, you will find me."

Jeremiah 29:13

"The Lord himself will fight for you. Just stay calm."

Exodus 14:14

"Each time he said, "My grace is all you need.

My power works best in weakness."

So now I am glad to boast about my weaknesses,

so that the power of Christ can work through me."

2 Corinthians 12:9

"Then Jesus said, "Come to me, all of you who are weary

And carry heavy burdens, and I will give you rest.

Take my yoke upon you. Let me teach you,

Because I am humble and gentle at heart,

And you will find rest for your souls.

For my yoke is easy to bear, and the burden I give you is light."

Matthew 11:28-30

"Come away with Me",

I hear You whisper to my heart.

"Seek My face in the stillness

Hear My voice in the quiet—"

"Remember who I AM;

The One who knows you by name.

I am waiting for your surrender

Of the burdens that weigh you down."

"Child, your strength is depleted."

Yes, Lord, I know it's true—
"But when you reach the end of yourself
There I am waiting for you."

"My arms are spread wide open;
My ears are keenly attuned—
I promise that when you seek Me, you'll find Me.
I'm waiting patiently before you."

"These battles that you're facing
Are beyond your meager frame.
But who can stand against a child of God!
One called by My holy name?"

"Come to me, weary one.
My burden is all you need.
Cast down the weight from your shoulders;
Lay them here at My feet."

"For I will fight in your stead.
You need only to be still.
I will deliver you from all your foes—
Trust Me—it will be well."

Oh Lord, wait for me in the stillness—

As I listen and seek Your face.

Pour Your strength into my spirit,

And hold me in Your Grace.

Reminders

"Look! The virgin will conceive a child!

She will give birth to a son,

And they will call Him Immanuel,

Which means "God is with us."'

Matthew 1:23

"The thief's purpose is to steal and kill and destroy.

My purpose is to give them a rich and satisfying life.

"I am the good shepherd.

The good shepherd sacrifices His life for the sheep."'

John 10:10-11

"But Jesus said, 'Let the children come to Me.

Don't stop them!

For the Kingdom of Heaven belongs to

Those who are like these little children."

Matthew 19:14

Melissa "Missy" Bishop

Like children engaged in late summer play,

Were the squirrels that joined me as I pondered.

Frolicking, jumping and chasing each other,

They sang and danced, chirped and skittered.

Up and down the tree trunks they roamed,

Chattering and tails twitching all the while.

And watching them scamper, hearing them cheep,

I found my weariness lifting—making me smile.

Today this grove called out to me,

In order to escape the chaos around.

And with a heart yearning for peace and calm,

There in the patchwork of sun it was found.

I went there hoping for a word from You,

A balm to heal these broken places.

Instead You used these quirky little creatures,

To lighten my heart—and bring liberation.

I know in my spirit You're always near,

And that You are found when I seek.

Lord, thank You for these little reminders,

That when I forget—there You'll be.

Realm of No Shadows

"I could ask the darkness to hide me and the light around me to become night—

But even in darkness I cannot hide from You. To You, the night shines

As bright as day. Darkness and light are the same to You."

Psalm 139:11-12

"We are pressed on every side by troubles, but we are not crushed.

We are perplexed, but not driven to despair."

2 Corinthians 4:8

"Yet what we suffer now is nothing compared to

The glory He will reveal to us later."

Romans 8:18

"No longer will there be a curse upon anything. For the throne of God

And of the Lamb will be there, and His servants will worship Him.

And they will see His face, and His name will be written on their foreheads.

And there will be no night there—no need for lamps or sun—

for the Lord God will shine on them. And they will reign forever and ever."

Revelation 22:3-5

Melissa "Missy" Bishop

The darkness keeps creeping--closing in;

As a hunter seeking its prey.

But even the darkness cannot hide,

To You, night shines bright as day.

The suffocating shadows keep grasping;

Trying to force me into the void--

But You promise: though crushed on every side,

In You, I shall not be destroyed.

For though the sufferings of this present age

Seem to abound and hem me in;

They cannot come near to the glory

To be revealed at this ages' end.

When the curse of sin forever is broken--

And Your Bride stands before Your throne;

Spotlessly clothed in the Robe of Redemption--

Your glory shining bright as the sun.

And in that Realm of no more shadows

You shall wipe all tears from my eyes.

The darkness no more to be remembered--

In that city illumined by the Lamb's pure light.

Melissa "Missy" Bishop

www.ingramcontent.com/pod-product-compliance
Lightning Source LLC
Chambersburg PA
CBHW081330090426
42737CB00017B/3078